Remembering Omaha

Jeffrey Spencer

Trade Paper Press

In this view west-northwest from 15th and Farnam streets in 1872, the new Omaha High School sits on the hilltop at upper-right. It was completed that year at a total cost of $225,000. The old Douglas County Court House, built in 1857, is visible in the center foreground, and just above it is Redick's Opera House on the northwest corner of 16th and Farnam streets, built by real-estate investor John I. Redick in 1870.

Remembering Omaha

Turner Publishing Company
200 4th Avenue North • Suite 950
Nashville, Tennessee 37219
(615) 255-2665

Remembering Omaha

www.turnerpublishing.com

Library of Congress Control Number: 2010924304

ISBN: 978-1-59652-650-1

Printed in the United States of America

10 11 12 13 14 15 16—0 9 8 7 6 5 4 3 2 1

Contents

The Exposition Building and Grand Opera House was an enormous brick structure built between 14th and 15th streets on Capitol Avenue in 1886-87. Costing in excess of $50,000 when completed, it could hold more than 5,000 persons. Many large productions were held here, including the traveling company of the New York Metropolitan Opera. The structure was destroyed by fire on December 4, 1894.

ACKNOWLEDGMENTS

This volume, *Remembering Omaha,* is the result of the cooperation and efforts of a number of organizations and individuals.

We would like to thank in particular the Durham Western Heritage Museum, the Omaha Public Library, and Joanne Ferguson Cavanaugh, librarian, Omaha Public Library.

—Jeffrey Spencer

This project represents countless hours of review and research. The researchers and writer have reviewed thousands of photographs. We greatly appreciate the generous assistance of the archives listed here, without whom this project could not have been completed.

The goal in publishing the work is to provide broader access to a set of extraordinary photographs. The aim is to inspire, provide perspective, and evoke insight that might assist officials and citizens, who together are responsible for determining Omaha's future. In addition, the book seeks to preserve the past with respect and reverence.

With the exception of touching up imperfections that have accrued with the passage of time and cropping where necessary, no changes have been made. The focus and clarity of many images are limited to the technology and the ability of the photographer at the time they were recorded.

We encourage readers to reflect as they explore Omaha, stroll along its streets, or wander its neighborhoods. It is the publisher's hope that in making use of this work, longtime residents will learn something new and that new residents will gain a perspective on where Omaha has been, so that each can contribute to its future.

—Todd Bottorff, Publisher

Preface

The history of the settlement and subsequent development of Omaha is an extension of the history of the American West, from the explorations of Lewis and Clark to the Manifest Destiny movement of the mid nineteenth century to the growth of railroads as the frontier pushed ever westward.

By July of 1804, the Corps of Discovery led by Lewis and Clark had reached the area where present-day Omaha is located. By 1820, the United States government had established its first permanent military post in the region, Fort Atkinson. Soon, settlers began moving into the area.

From 1845 until 1848, during the Mormon migration, the Winter Quarters site was established approximately six miles north of the later town site of Omaha. At one time, as many as 15,000 "temporary" residents lived there, resting along their journey to the basin of the Great Salt Lake. Many elected to stay.

On December 14, 1853, Senator Augustus C. Dodge of Iowa introduced a bill in the United States Senate to organize the Territory of Nebraska. After much discussion and delay, this bill was finally ratified and signed into law by President Franklin Pierce on May 30, 1854. The next month, a treaty was ratified between the United States and the Otoe, Missouri, and Omaha Indians, which gave land title in the area to the government and allowed for settlement to commence. On July 4, 1854, the first official gathering took place on what was to be the town site of Omaha, and many people consider this date to be the founding of the city. Immediately, large numbers of people began crossing the Missouri River from the Iowa side, and took up claims in what was then known as Omaha City.

By 1857, the new town boasted 1,700 residents, and the Nebraska Territorial Legislature granted a petition for the incorporation of Omaha as a city. That same year, a great financial panic took hold in the East, which halted the growth of the new town. Almost two-thirds of the residents moved away, and most banks and businesses went bankrupt. The discovery of gold in Colorado in 1859 breathed new life into the community as

Omaha became an important supply station for those going west. In 1863, President Abraham Lincoln established the route of the transcontinental railroad through Omaha. From that point forward, the destiny of the community was assured.

Due to its central geographic location, and sitting beside the great inland waterway of the Missouri River, Omaha was poised to become an important trade and transportation center. This became more evident with the completion of the Union Pacific railroad in 1868. The decades of the 1870s and 1880s saw tremendous growth in the area. The temporary, pioneer atmosphere gave way to a community of substance and prosperity. Fine homes, schools, and public buildings were constructed.

In 1893, the country was thrown into another serious financial depression. The Midwest was especially affected. After several years of bad weather, crop failures, and a general decline in market demand, the situation had become critical. Business leaders in the community began trying to devise a plan to revitalize the local economy. They decided to host a World's Fair in Omaha, to be held during the summer and fall of 1898. This became the Trans-Mississippi and International Exposition and Indian Congress. For the first time, international attention was focused on Omaha, and the community rose to the occasion. This was by far the most important and significant event to take place in Omaha.

By 1900, Omaha was moving forward into the new century with a population well in excess of 100,000. After the decline of the railroad, a new economic force began to emerge with the establishment of the adjacent community of South Omaha and the meatpacking and processing business. The Union Stockyards Company, established in 1883, eventually controlled 22 large packing companies and employed more than 30,000 workers. To fill those jobs, Omaha became a key destination for immigrants coming to America. Although Germans and Irish were the predominant groups, immigrants from almost every country in Europe could be found living and working here.

The Omaha of today is moving forward in many significant ways. Commercial development is very active, with many large corporations establishing offices here. Two significant events took place in 2004: The Lewis and Clark Bicentennial Commemoration and the Omaha 150th Birthday Sesquicentennial Celebration. The city is moving ahead into the twenty-first century.

Omaha is fortunate to possess a very extensive visual archive of its history and development. From those priceless resources, we have gathered the historic views presented in this collection. These photographic images open a window through which we can glimpse a view of Omaha as it grew and became the city it is today. We trust that you will enjoy looking at this collection as much as we have enjoyed putting it together and bringing it to you.

—Jeffrey Spencer

Plans were approved for the construction of a new Union Station at 10th and Mason street in 1929. Noted Los Angeles architect Gilbert Stanley Underwood was awarded the commission. When completed early in 1931 at a cost of $3.5 million, it was considered one of the finest examples of Art Deco architecture in the country. This is the new depot as it appeared in January 1931.

Frontier on the Missouri

(1860s–1889)

The Missouri River Transfer Company's side-wheel steamboat *H. C. Nutt* in 1866. Prior to the completion of the first railroad bridge in 1872, this boat was moored in the Missouri River and used to ferry railroad cars between Council Bluffs, Iowa, and Omaha. In the winter when the river was frozen, temporary tracks were laid across the ice, so that the trains might cross.

Shown shortly after its completion in 1867, the Caldwell Block was a business area located on the south side of Douglas between 13th and 14th streets. This block contained the Academy of Music, the Omaha National Bank, the Omaha *Republican* newspaper and job printer, a restaurant, a book bindery, and a photographic gallery. The Academy of Music, which had a large auditorium, was the only permanent venue for stage productions in Omaha until the opening of Boyd's Opera House in 1881.

Douglas Street to the east about 1869, from approximately 18th Street. Many of the first wooden pioneer structures have already been replaced by more substantial brick buildings. On the left, is the German Catholic Church at the northwest corner of 16th and Douglas streets. This church was dedicated on Christmas Day 1868. Across the river in the distance is the growing city of Council Bluffs, Iowa.

This image of the Nebraska Territorial Capitol located in Capitol Square at 20th and Dodge streets, dates from about 1869. It was in use as the territorial capitol from approximately 1858 to 1867. The building was 137 feet by 93 feet, with the supreme court, library, and government offices on the first floor. The legislative and governor's offices were on the second floor. In 1867, when Nebraska became a state, the capital was moved to Lincoln. In 1869, the building and grounds were presented to Omaha. By 1872, it had been torn down and replaced by Omaha High School.

The Missouri River Bridge at Omaha was completed in March 1872, when this view was recorded. Each of its eleven spans was 250 feet long. The approach on the Omaha side was situated at the foot of Mason Street. The bridge was rebuilt after being struck by a tornado in 1877. It was rebuilt again and reinforced in 1916.

The Tremont House, one of the first hotels in the city, opened in October 1856, on the south side of Douglas between 13th and 14th streets. It was operated by William F. Sweesy and Aaron Root until 1865. At that time, the hotel was sold and the building moved to the southeast corner of 16th and Capitol streets. This photograph was made about 1878, after it had moved to the new location.

The City Hotel, shown here around 1877, on the west side of 10th Street between Farnam and Harney was Omaha's second hotel. Prior to 1860, there were few brick structures because there were no brickyards here. Building materials had to be brought across the river from Council Bluffs, Iowa.

Druggist Julius A. Roeder's business was located on the southeast corner of 16th and Webster streets. Next door is the Union Pacific building, 621 North 16th Street, home to the Union Pacific Railroad Market, a company store operated by the railroad for the benefit of its employees. This photograph was taken about 1879.

This view of Metz Brothers Beer Hall, 510–512 South 10th Street, was taken in 1879. Metz Brothers Brewing Company was one of the earliest breweries in Omaha, with headquarters at 6th and Leavenworth. Germans were the largest immigrant group in Omaha, and brothers Charles and Fred Metz arrived early on to establish their business. At one time, there were nine large breweries operating in the city.

General view of Omaha to the northwest in 1879, taken from the tower of Omaha High School on Capitol Hill. Creighton College, at upper-left, is Creighton University today, one of the leading Catholic universities in the United States. This view gives a clear idea of the rapid development of the city during this period.

This view, taken in the early 1880s, shows the Paxton Hotel, located on the southwest corner of 14th and Farnam streets. When it opened in 1882, it was considered Omaha's finest hotel. It was torn down in 1927 to make way for the elegant New Paxton Hotel, which opened June 26, 1929.

Creighton College, a private Catholic institution of higher learning, opened in Omaha on September 2, 1879. This photograph taken about 1892 shows the original brick structure which housed the school. It was located at 25th and California streets. Another wing was added later. Today, Creighton University ranks as one of the outstanding private universities in the United States.

The Sheely Block, 419 South 15th Street. This office building was designed by prominent local architects Mendelssohn, Fisher and Lawrie and was built in 1887 at the northeast corner of 15th and Howard streets. The original cost was $116,000, and at the time the structure was considered one of the finest business blocks in the city. This is the building as it looked in the 1890s.

Coming of Age

(1890–1900)

Omaha High School was constructed between 1869 and 1872 at a total cost of $225,000. This picture was taken about 1895. Designed by Chicago architect G. R. Randall, it was built on Capitol Hill, the site of the Nebraska Territorial Capitol. On November 1, 1875, when President Ulysses S. Grant and the First Lady visited, they came to this building to meet a large group of Omaha schoolchildren. This structure was torn down after 1900, when a new high school was built on the same site. Today, Omaha's Central High School occupies this location.

The Douglas County Court House, designed by E. E. Meyers of Detroit, as it appeared in the 1890s. The wooden retaining wall holds back earth being removed as the street was lowered to cut down the hill on which the courthouse was built. The location was between 17th and 18th streets on Farnam. It was completed in 1885 at a cost of $200,000 and opened with a large public reception that year on May 28. The building was razed in 1908 for the construction of a new courthouse at the same location.

On May 13, 1891, President Benjamin Harrison and the First Lady visited Omaha. The presidential party proceeded by carriage to 17th and Farnam streets, where a speaker's platform had been constructed. This large crowd gathered in front of the Douglas County Court House to hear him. Later, a public reception was held in the atrium court of the Bee Building. Afterwards, the president visited Omaha High School and Creighton College before returning to Union Station.

On April 1, 1887, the Omaha and Council Bluffs Railway and Bridge Company was organized to build a street railway bridge across the Missouri River at Douglas Street between Omaha and Council Bluffs, Iowa. The new bridge and an electric streetcar motor line opened on November 1, 1888. This view was recorded in the 1890s, looking toward Omaha from the Council Bluffs side. The bridge stood until the late 1960s.

Omaha, viewed north along 17th Street. On the right is the new United States Post Office and Customs House. Trinity Episcopal Cathedral appears at far-left and to the right of that is the First Presbyterian Church.

The Millard Hotel on the northeast corner of 13th and Douglas was a five-story, brick building that opened to the public in July 1882. Considered one of the best hotels in Omaha, it was the site of many community events. Although touted as "absolutely fireproof," it was destroyed in a spectacular blaze on February 8, 1933, when temperatures reached 15 degrees below zero. Seven Omaha fire fighters lost their lives, and 22 others were injured.

The Executive Officers of the Trans-Mississippi Exposition, meeting in executive session at the Omaha Club on 20th and Douglas streets in 1898. Left to right: Freeman P. Kirkendall, Edward E. Bruce, Abraham L. Reed, Chairman Zachary T. Lindsey, Secretary John A. Wakefield, Edward Rosewater, William N. Babcock, and President Gurdon W. Wattles.

This was a residential street in the affluent "Gold Coast" neighborhood where many prominent families relocated, beginning near the end of the nineteenth century. The conical tower of the Charles Turner residence is visible in the middle of the block. Today, this area contains many of Omaha's architectural landmarks.

The first United States Post Office building in Omaha was located on the southwest corner of 15th and Dodge streets. Construction began in 1870 and was completed in 1874 at a cost of $300,000. It was built entirely of limestone. When a new and much larger post office opened in 1898, this structure became the Army Building, utilized for the headquarters of the U.S. Army Department of the Platte. It was later razed to provide the site for a new Federal Building in 1930.

A typical interior view of a late-nineteenth-century grocery, Larson's Store, at 27th and Lake streets. At the time, almost all businesses providing goods and services were small, independent, neighborhood establishments such as this. The bins and barrels were used for holding various commodities. Individual packaging was rare.

The Woodman and Ritchie Company, located on the corner of 17th and Nicholas streets. This large grain elevator with a capacity of 600,000 bushels opened September 1, 1890, operated by Clark Woodman and Frank E. Ritchie. The elevator was 140 feet tall, one of the largest and most successful in the area. After the death of Woodman in 1891, Ritchie continued the business as sole proprietor. This photograph was made in the late 1890s.

Portable bandstand being moved in Hanscom Park, 32nd and Woolworth streets, in the late 1890s. Hanscom Park is the oldest park in Omaha, established in the fall of 1872. It was named for pioneer Andrew Jackson Hanscom, one of the original donors of a 57.5-acre tract of land. With a lagoon, a large pavilion, and numerous walkways decorated with artistic arrangements of plants and flowers, it was an oasis of beauty in early Omaha.

Klopp, Bartlett and Company was a large commercial printing company. Shortly after Klopp and Bartlett took over the business in 1885, the premises were badly damaged by fire, and they relocated to the building shown here at 1114 Farnam Street. Continuing to expand, they were soon also operating a large book bindery and a lithography department. This is their press room in the late 1890s.

A large pavilion with striped awnings stood in Hanscom Park, 32nd and Woolworth, in the late 1890s. Band concerts held in an elegant bandstand, picnics, fishing in the lagoon, and winter ice-skating in the park were all sources of entertainment for local citizens.

A view of downtown Omaha as it appeared in the late 1890s, west on Farnam Street from 14th. The Barker Building, southwest corner of 15th and Farnam, is in the center. Just to its west is the Henshaw Hotel. Pedestrians, horse-drawn vehicles, and a streetcar share the brick-paved streets.

St. John's Collegiate Church was the second structure built on the campus of Creighton College. This Romanesque-style church at 2506 California Street, built of gray stone, is one of the most beautiful edifices in the city. The interior contains many memorials to members of the Creighton family. This image was made about 1890.

This neighborhood grocery store was owned and operated by Henry Moeller, located on the northwest corner of 13th and Jones streets. It is typical of the small businesses which served the needs of local residents. This photograph dates to approximately 1890.

Around 1892, the Falconer residence at 1821 Douglas Street was lowered to the new street level, which had been excavated as part of the municipal engineering project to reduce the steep grade of Omaha's streets.

An 1892 view of the street-lowering project shows residences along Douglas Street at 18th. The street obviously was lowered a considerable amount. These projects were undertaken to allow for the installation of street railway service, which could not run easily on steep grades.

Street regrading was the first large-scale engineering project in the city. Many independent contractors were employed to work on various sections. This crew is working near 2420 Harney Street in the early 1890s.

An audience watches cavalry maneuvers in the late 1890s at Fort Omaha, a military post north of the central city. Tents have been set up beside the parade ground. Established in 1868, the post was administered by the U.S. Army Department of the Platte during the Indian Wars. Today, many original buildings house the North Campus of Omaha's Metropolitan Community College at 30th and Fort streets.

Army horses stand beyond a large tent set up beside the parade ground at Fort Omaha, 30th and Fort streets, during cavalry maneuvers in the late 1890s. This fort is now the site of the North Campus of Metropolitan Community College.

A view of the United States Government Building at the Trans-Mississippi and International Exposition and Indian Congress, held in Omaha June 1 through October 31, 1898. This building was located at the west end of a large man-made "lagoon," which was 8 city blocks long and more than 300 feet wide.

This "Mini Roller Coaster" was one of the Midway attractions at the Trans-Mississippi Exposition. Many such small concessions were transported by rail to the fairgrounds where the operators leased space. Admission for most of the attractions was 5 or 10 cents, and the operators had to pay a percentage of their profits to the Exposition Company in addition to the rental fee. A sign advertises, "This Magnificent Machine for Sale."

The main entrance to the Agricultural Building, Trans-Mississippi Exposition, 1898. One of the large "palaces" which surrounded the Lagoon, or Grand Court area, it was more than 400 feet long and about 150 feet wide. This building was designed by the famous architect Cass Gilbert. It contained many exhibits related to agricultural production.

General Electric Company hosted this large exhibit in the Machinery and Electricity Building, located on the Grand Court. Electric power was in its infancy and was a noted feature of the Trans-Mississippi Exposition, which was one of the first large-scale events in the United States to be entirely illuminated with electric lighting. Thomas Edison himself designed the electrical features of the Omaha fair.

The North Midway at the Trans-Mississippi Exposition. The Cyclorama on the left featured a large, panoramic painting depicting the first naval battle between ironclads. In the upper center of the photo is the Pabst Pavilion, which was operated by the Pabst Brewery as a restaurant and beer garden. To its right is the outline of the Giant See-Saw, a very popular feature of the Midway.

The Cyclorama on the North Midway held a large, circular panoramic painting of the famous naval battle between the ironclads USS *Monitor* and CSS *Virginia* (formerly named USS *Merrimac*) at Hampton Roads during the Civil War. Patrons entered the enclosure and walked around an elevated wooden platform to view the painting. The white signs outside entice viewers with admission prices that are "½ Rate To-day."

The Trans-Mississippi Exposition featured more than 5,000 individual exhibits. This one for Blatz Beer would have been in the Manufacturers Building located on the Grand Court, one of the largest exhibition buildings. All the structures were built using temporary materials. A combination of plaster, ground hemp (rope) fiber, and Portland cement were mixed together to form a substance called "staff." This was formed in sections using molds and attached to a wooden superstructure.

Tuesday, August 2, 1898, was "Flower Day" at the Trans-Mississippi Exposition. About 40 horse-drawn vehicles were transformed into parade floats, decorated entirely with fresh flowers. This proved to be a very popular event.

The Giant See-Saw located on the North Midway was one of the most popular attractions. This concession was brought to Omaha from Nashville after the close of the 1897 Tennessee Centennial Exposition. For an admission of 10 cents, passengers were elevated almost 200 feet above the ground. Several couples were married in the cars as they were raised to the highest point.

The display of the American Wringer Company, located in the Manufacturers Building, is an example of the type of exhibit that was very popular with those who attended the fair. World's Fairs were considered important venues for information and education. Modern technology was eagerly sought after by those who came to view these exhibits.

The Streets of Cairo was a large Midway attraction located on the Bluff Tract. It was a conglomeration of "Eastern" exoticism and architecture. The cafe, shown here, offered unusual teas and other Oriental treats for the enjoyment of fairgoers. These displays were very popular, as most people in the region had never traveled outside the United States.

The Streets Of All Nations on the North Midway was an even larger assemblage of exotic designs, displays, and entertainment. For an admission charge of 15 cents, visitors could pass through an imposing Egyptian-style entrance to view a wide assortment of displays. Camel rides, exotic dancers, impromptu athletic competitions, varied native costumes, and performances in the Streets Of All Nations Theatre were among the attractions waiting inside.

The Trans-Mississippi Exposition was a very large event, and security was an ongoing concern. Besides special guards for the United States Government Building, there was a general security staff employed by the Exposition Company. The Chief of the Exposition Guards and his staff are shown here. The Exposition had more than 2.5 million visitors during its period of operation.

August 4, 1898, was "Indian Day," and this parade of Native Americans marched through the fairgrounds. One of the outstanding features of the Exposition was the Indian Congress, which brought together 500 Native Americans, representing many different tribes and nations. This was the last time that such a gathering took place before most were resettled on reservations established by the federal government.

Lake Nakoma, originally named "Cut-Off Lake," formed in 1877 as the result of a flood which caused the Missouri River to reroute its channel. In 1908, this lake was renamed Carter Lake, in honor of pioneer Levi P. Carter. At that time, his widow donated $50,000 for the improvement of the area as a recreational facility.

A New Century

(1901–1920)

Looking south-southeast from the intersection of 15th and Dodge streets. The cupola visible at upper-center is atop the Continental Block, a large office building located at the northeast corner of 15th and Douglas.

The street railway viaduct on O Street in the vicinity of 33rd in South Omaha in the early 1900s. Beyond it are numerous meatpacking houses of the Union Stock Yards Company, the economic backbone of the community for many years.

The working area behind the tellers' cages at the Omaha National Bank, 212 South 13th Street.

The pavilion at Elmwood Park was one of the first structures in Omaha built of cast concrete. Originally an open-air structure, it was closed to the public in 1939. Later, it was repaired and enclosed. In 1987, $100,000 from a special bond issue was expended to refurbish it. This photograph was taken around 1905.

The Paxton Block, as it appeared around 1905. Located at 16th and Farnam streets, this large office building was financed by Omaha capitalist William A. Paxton, whose name was associated with many local enterprises. He would usually provide the funds and take in other minority partners who would then manage the various businesses. Paxton died in Omaha in 1907.

Pavilion at Riverside Park, 3625 South 10th Street, about 1905. This outdoor pavilion was constructed of wooden architectural elements which had been salvaged from the Boys and Girls Building at the 1898 Trans-Mississippi Exposition.

The Riverside Park pavilion, about 1905. Located in South Omaha, this park was a very popular location, featuring a lagoon and the first zoo in Omaha.

A crowd of well-dressed citizens enjoys an afternoon picnic at Riverside Park about 1905, with the park pavilion in the background.

This view, taken about 1905 looking east down Farnam Street from the Douglas County Court House at 18th Street, shows the Omaha Building, a large office building, on the left. At left-center is the Paxton Block on the northeast corner of 16th and Farnam streets.

A crew of road builders paves South 24th Street with bricks, around 1904. The streetcar in the background transported workers to the site. Prior to 1890, many of Omaha's streets had no paving at all. When it rained, they became rivers of mud. The earliest form of paving was with wooden blocks. The blocks did not last long, but some of the early brick streets are still in use today.

The Omaha National Bank at 208 South 13th Street, in 1909. This substantial, six-story structure was built in 1882. The bank, which opened for business in Omaha July 2, 1866, outgrew this location and shortly thereafter moved to the New York Life Building at 17th and Farnam streets.

This view of downtown Omaha, July 13, 1909, shows the intersection of 16th and Farnam streets, in the heart of the main business district. The United States National Bank is in the center. To its right is People's Store, and beside it banners proclaim the recently completed store of J. L. Brandeis and Sons. The U.S. Post Office tower is visible farther down the street. At this time of transition, electric streetcars, gasoline-powered automobiles, and horse-drawn vehicles all traveled the streets between crowded sidewalks.

A photograph taken about 1910 of the large, steel hangar built at Fort Omaha, 30th and Fort streets, in 1907 for dirigible experiments. After the United States entered World War I, this facility was utilized by the U.S. Signal Corps to establish the Fort Omaha Balloon School. Eighteen hundred men received training there to become the "Eyes of the Army."

Elmwood Park on West Dodge Street was established when pioneer Lyman Richardson and others made a donation of 55 acres of land in 1890. The City of Omaha soon added additional property, and by 1895 the total expanded land area was 210 acres. Today, this is one of the most beautiful parks in Omaha. This image shows a couple driving a Velie automobile through it around 1910.

The lily pond in Riverview Park, 3625 South 10th Street, about 1910. Visiting one of Omaha's many parks was an enjoyable weekend activity for residents, and this park was especially popular, with its beautiful natural setting and many interesting landscape features.

The Guarantee Laundry, 1468 South 16th Street, was owned and operated by Leonard C. Heine. Laundry workers have assembled for a group portrait.

The New York Life Building at 17th and Farnam streets, as it appeared about 1910, soon after the Omaha National Bank had moved its offices there. Completed in 1889 at a cost of $750,000, this ten-story building was Omaha's first "skyscraper." It was designed by the prestigious New York City architectural firm of McKim, Meade and White. An eleventh floor was added in 1920. This structure today is one of the most important architectural and historic landmarks in the city.

Disaster struck Omaha on Easter Sunday, March 23, 1913, at about 6:00 P.M., when a tornado moved through the city. Approximately 185 people were killed. The ruins in this image are what remained of the home of Judge W. W. Slabaugh at 4912 Underwood Avenue in Dundee.

Livestock pens at the Union Stockyards Company in South Omaha about 1908, in the vicinity of 33rd and O streets. The Armour Packing Company appears near the top. In 1887, Philip D. Armour first became involved in the meatpacking business in Omaha. His reorganized company built their own large plant there in 1898. By the beginning of the twentieth century, Armour and Company was one of the four largest meat processors in Omaha.

In this west-facing photo from about 1910, the steps of the Douglas County Court House are in the foreground, along with one section of the AK-SAR-BEN welcome arch which spanned Farnam at 18th Street. In the middle of the block, across from the business college, is the Wolfe Electric Company. Down the street, The Bachelor's was a saloon and billiards hall.

The pavilion at Miller Park, 2707 Redick Avenue, as it appeared about 1910. The 78 acres of this park were obtained by the city in 1893. It later featured a golf course, a fountain, beautiful walkways, and gardens and was considered one of the finest parks in the city. It was named in honor of pioneer Dr. George L. Miller, who had served as the first president of the Omaha Board of Park Commissioners.

Elmwood Park, located west of Dodge Street (802 South 60th Street) opened its golf course in 1916. This has always been a popular municipal course due to its accessibility and convenient midtown location. By the 1960s, nearly 30,000 rounds of golf were played annually.

The Blackstone Hotel at 302 South 36th Street as it appeared shortly after it opened in 1916. One of the finest residential hotels in the city, it was built in the prosperous "Gold Coast" neighborhood, where many of the most prominent families in the city lived. It closed in 1976 and was later renovated for use as a commercial office building.

The ornate old city hall building on the corner of 18th and Farnam streets was designed by Omaha architect Charles F. Biendorf and completed in 1890 at a total cost of $550,000. A tower on the southeast corner rose to a height of nearly 200 feet. Construction flaws necessitated removal of the tower in 1919. Remodeled extensively in 1950, the building later became obsolete. The city sold the site in 1966, and in March of that year, the structure was torn down.

AK-SAR-BEN was an important community service organization founded in Omaha in 1895. Each year, it produced an elaborate parade, often using electrified floats. This parade on September 23, 1920, was photographed on Farnam Street between 16th and 18th streets.

A main attraction every year was the "electrical parades" put on by the Knights of AK-SAR-BEN. This float, titled "Romeo and Juliet," was part of the September 1920 parade, which had the theme "Famous Love Tales." Thousands of people lined the downtown streets to view the parades every fall.

This picture was taken March 31, 1920, facing north-northwest from the top of the Woodmen of the World Building on the corner of 14th and Farnam, which was Omaha's tallest building at the time. The U.S. Post Office is to the upper left and at upper-right is the large headquarters building of the Union Pacific Railroad at 15th and Dodge streets.

THE GATE CITY

(1921–1939)

This photograph, facing southwest on Dodge at 17th Street, was taken in the early 1920s during excavation for the Medical Arts Building. The building was finally completed in 1926 after being plagued by delays and financial difficulties. Containing 17 floors, it included commercial space, medical offices, and even a 500-seat auditorium. A gem of Art Deco architecture, it was the last major commission undertaken by noted Omaha architect Thomas R. Kimball. It was torn down in 1999.

The $400,000 AK-SAR-BEN Coliseum as it appeared shortly after it was completed in 1928. It became the location of all the organization's functions for many years. Located at 64th and Center streets, it had a capacity of 7,200. The coliseum was torn down in 2005, after the property had been sold for redevelopment.

The Fontenelle Hotel, photographed in 1928 at the height of its popularity, was located at 1806 Douglas Street and opened with great celebration in 1915. Prominent architect Thomas R. Kimball designed it for the Douglas Hotel Company. For many years, the Fontenelle served as Omaha's premier hotel, hosting many important events. After closing in 1971, it was unoccupied for several years. When redevelopment plans were not forthcoming, it was torn down in 1983.

The newly completed Livestock Exchange Building at 2900 O Plaza in 1926. Designed by prominent Omaha architect George B. Prinz, this structure remains today the most distinctive landmark in South Omaha. Built by Peter Kiewit and Sons Construction Company at a cost of $1 million, it was for many years a symbol of the national role played by Omaha in the livestock and meat-processing industry. Recently, it was redeveloped for commercial and residential use.

The Dundee Theatre, 4952 Dodge Street, soon after it was built in 1925. Originally a stage theater used for vaudeville and live performances, it was converted to a movie house in the 1930s. An important landmark in the Dundee area, it is considered to be the last neighborhood theater still operating in Omaha.

Looking slightly northwest around 52nd Street and Underwood Avenue in the Dundee neighborhood, this photograph was taken in June 1926. Lake George in the foreground—named for the George brothers who developed the area—was later filled in. Dundee was an affluent residential area, which at one time had been a separate town. It was annexed into the city of Omaha in 1915.

In the early 1920s, this photograph was taken from the rooftop of the Union Pacific Railroad's headquarters building, looking east along Dodge from 14th Street. The Dodge Hotel is on the corner. The jobbing and warehouse district is visible at upper-right.

The downtown commercial district, south from 16th and Dodge streets in 1921. On the right side of the street, at the upper center, is the First National Bank building at 16th and Farnam. To its right, the tall, white building is J. L. Brandies and Sons department store at 16th and Douglas streets. Across Douglas is the Boston Store and beside it Hayden Brothers Department Store. In the left foreground is the Hotel Neville, 107 North 16th Street, which advertised itself as “a modern home away from home in the heart of the business district.”

Howard Street west from 8th Street in the wholesale district or "Jobbers Canyon" as it was known, in 1921. The "canyon" was formed by the continual line of large warehouse buildings that housed manufactured goods. A truck from the Omaha Printing (and office supplies) Company is visible in the foreground, while the Jicase Plow Works Company and the water tower for Wright & Wilhelmy appear beyond the box cars. The warehouses were built to have direct access to the rail line. Several of the remaining warehouse buildings in this area have been redeveloped into residential properties.

This picture was taken from the roof of the Blackstone Hotel, looking east on Farnam Street near 36th Street in 1921. Toward the top left of the picture is the First Presbyterian Church, built in 1917. Several of the large, elegant mansions of prosperous families in what was called the Gold Coast neighborhood are also visible. In the foreground, a lot is being redeveloped for commercial use.

The west side of 16th Street at Jackson in May 1929. At left is the Castle Hotel. In the center foreground is the bus depot, with the Beaton Drug Company located in a corner of that structure. Horse-drawn delivery wagons like the one shown were increasingly scarce as the 1920s came to a close.

The Paxton and Gallagher Grocery Company was founded in Omaha in 1882. One of its most popular products was Butter-Nut Coffee, which was roasted and packaged here. This 1931 photograph shows one of the company's delivery trucks. The Paxton and Gallagher Company existed until 1958, when it was sold and absorbed into the Swanson Food Company.

The AK-SAR-BEN racetrack and grandstand, as it appeared in 1935. On September 14, 1920, the racetrack was officially dedicated at the new property on west Center Street. In 1921, the large grandstand seen here was completed. It held more than 6,500 spectators. A complete horse-racing program was available, which included trotting, pacing, and running.

August 1933, facing north on 15th Street from the Carlton Hotel located on the corner of 15th and Howard streets. On the left is the sign at the back of the Orpheum Theatre. Beyond it is the Redick Tower at the northwest corner of 15th and Harney streets, and to the right of that, the Barker Building, at the southwest corner of 15th and Farnam streets.

This is a November 1939 interior view of the bar and cafe owned by William Gofta at 4940 South 26th Street. It is typical of the neighborhood gathering places which were popular at that time. This South Omaha establishment was frequented by livestock commission men.

Interior of the imposing Main Waiting Room in Union Station, at 10th and Mason streets. This view was recorded at the time the station was completed in January 1931. This great hall was 72 feet wide and 160 feet long, with a ceiling rising to a height of 60 feet. The station closed in 1971, and after remaining empty for a time, became home to the Durham Western Heritage Museum, still housed there today.

Two of the delivery cars for the Carl S. Baum Drug Company in 1935. This locally owned firm was located at 5001 Underwood Avenue in the Dundee neighborhood.

The interior of Walgreen's Drug Store at 1624 Harney Street, one of two locations in Omaha around 1935. The other was at 4902 Dodge Street. This company has continued to grow and prosper, with stores throughout Omaha today.

Brothers Charles D. and Clyde A. Blubaugh operated a full-service tire business at 1819–1821 Cuming Street, shown here in 1935.

The main entrance of the Orpheum Theatre at 409 South 16th Street, when the 1935 *Bride of Frankenstein* movie was showing. On this site in 1895, John Creighton built the Creighton Theatre. In 1898, when it became a vaudeville house associated with the Orpheum Circuit, the name was changed to the Orpheum Theatre. This theater closed on April 25, 1926, and the original building was torn down. A new theater was built, shown here.

When the new Orpheum Theatre opened in 1927, it was truly magnificent. The main entrance had been changed from 15th Street to 16th, and the auditorium could seat 3,000. These are advertisements for attractions that were coming after New Year's Day 1934.

The Mercantile Storage and Warehouse Building at 711 South 11th Street, photographed in the 1930s. Constructed in two phases during 1919-20, it originally had six stories, but three more were added in 1920. It was used as a wholesale warehouse for several large grocery companies. Completely renovated in 2001, it was readapted for residential use.

Harkert's Holsum Hamburgers at 16th and Dodge streets in 1935. Walter E. Harkert started his business in Omaha in 1925, selling sandwiches to people attending the American Legion National Convention. Later, he opened a series of small restaurants, eventually owning 21 locations. During the Depression, he offered a cup of coffee and a hamburger for 10 cents. He retired and sold his business in October 1967. The last of his restaurants, under new ownership, closed in February 1974.

McFayden Stewart Company was an automobile and truck business at 1923 Harney Street. In this 1935 photograph, a fleet of delivery trucks belonging to the J. L. Brandeis and Sons Department Store sit in front of the dealership. McFayden Stewart later became McFayden Ford and was in business in Omaha for many years.

The new Technical High School was built at 33rd and Cuming streets in 1923. At the time of its construction, it was considered one of the finest school buildings in the entire country. It cost $3.5 million to build and had a capacity of more than 3,000 students. This 1934 photograph shows the marching band.

The Barnsdall Symphony Orchestra performing in Omaha in November 1930, sponsored by local radio station KOIL. This was the second radio station licensed in Omaha and began broadcasting on July 10, 1925. The "OIL" in the call letters "KOIL" indicated the fact that the station was owned by the Mona Motor Oil Company.

The clubhouse of the Happy Hollow Club at 1701 South 105th Street in June 1931. Originally founded in 1907, the club decided to relocate in 1922. A large tract of land in West Omaha was obtained, and local architect Harry Lawrie was commissioned to design an elegant and spacious clubhouse. A grand opening celebration on May 25, 1925, drew about 600 people. The Happy Hollow Club remains today one of Omaha's most outstanding features.

Reaching Toward the Future

(1940–1960s)

Glaser's Provisions, located at 5036 South 26th Street in South Omaha, was operated by Fred H. Glaser, who was engaged in the wholesale meat business. He supplied schools, hotels, and restaurants. His fleet of delivery trucks was photographed outside the business in June 1941.

The Petersen and Michelsen Hardware Store, 4916 South 24th Street in South Omaha, carried a wide range of products and supplies. This interior view was taken in December 1947.

In November 1948, when this photo was taken, ladies' admission was free on Friday nights at the Roseland Theater, and men were urged to bring their girl, their mother, or their wife. Located at 4939 South 24th Street, in the heart of the South Omaha business district, it was originally built in 1922 by entrepreneur James W. Murphy and designed by South Omaha architect James T. Allen. It closed in 1950. A year later, Murphy converted the building into the Roseland Arcade and indoor shopping center. The Roseland Redevelopment Corporation later turned it into apartments.

During a 1941 Army Day exercise at Fort Omaha, an announcer from Radio Station KOIL was photographed broadcasting live beside one of the barracks.

Omaha joined the rest of America in celebrating the end of World War II on V-J (Victory over Japan) Day in August 1945. This image shows the crowded corner of 16th and Farnam, littered with paper debris from the joyous celebrations. The United States National Bank building, with F. W. Woolworth on its ground floor, stands to the left, across 16th from Goldstein-Chapman's Department Store.

During the 1948 presidential campaign, Republican candidate Thomas Dewey of New York made a stop in Omaha. Here, he is being interviewed on live radio by Bud Thorpe from Radio Station KOIL.

"Nat Towles Great Orchestra: 14 Southern Gentlemen," with their touring bus in September 1940. The son of New Orleans bassist Phil "Charlie" Towles, Nat was a significant influence on the development of jazz. Born in 1905, he formed his first band, the Creole Harmony Kings, in 1923. He established himself permanently in Omaha at the Dreamland Ballroom in 1936. He worked through the 1950s and retired to California.

President Harry S. Truman visited Boys Town in June 1948, while in Omaha to dedicate the World War II Memorial. To his left is Monsignor Francis P. Schmidt, music director. Patrick Norton, general manager and nephew of Boys Town founder Edward J. Flanagan, is on his right. Father Flanagan had died the previous month in Germany; President Truman had asked him to go there for discussions on European children left homeless and orphaned by the war.

Harney Street, west from 15th in October 1951. The 12-story, Art Deco Redick Tower office building at right, 1504 Harney Street, was built in 1930 at a cost of $453,000. To its left are a tavern and a sporting goods store. The large building farther to the left is the Regis Hotel, at 314 South 16th Street.

A city engineering project in August 1951, digging a trench in front of city hall at 18th and Farnam streets. The Douglas County Court House is south across the street, and to the west, the Wellington and Keen hotels.

Looking north from the area of 16th and Harney streets, August 12, 1954. Beyond the Montgomery Ward Department Store is Carmen's. This was a women's clothing store operated by Reuben W. Natelson at 412 South 16th Street. Next to it is the Regis Hotel, followed by the First National Bank. The large banners proclaim Omaha's 100th Birthday, which was celebrated that year.

The sidewalks in front of the S. S. Kresge Company store at 402 South 16th Street were crowded on August 18, 1954.

The second Hanscom Park Methodist Church building, constructed in the fall of 1892 at a cost of $20,000, was located at 1345 South 29th Street. The congregation later relocated to 4444 Frances Street, where they continue to meet today. This picture of the church was taken in June 1959.

An interior view of Craddock's Bicycle Shop. This shop was located at 5901 North 30th Street, in the Minne Lusa neighborhood.

Automobiles, city buses, and an electric streetcar at the intersection of South 24th and N streets in South Omaha, September 1951. The bus line here carried workers to and from their jobs in the large packing houses. On the left is the Stockyards National Bank, in the heart of the commercial district.

In April 1952, the Missouri River began to rise ominously, causing stress on the levees at Omaha. The mayor declared an emergency. Thousands of community volunteers joined military units in an effort to reinforce the levees and raise them with sand bags. On April 17, the river crested in Omaha at 30.25 feet, the highest level ever recorded. Although there was widespread damage in the area, the reinforced levees held.

At the time this aerial view of Omaha was taken in 1955, the population of the city had risen to well over 250,000. In the center is the rapidly developing downtown business district and above that, the Missouri River. Across the river is Council Bluffs, Iowa.

St. Catherine's Hospital at 8th Street and Forest Avenue in February 1966. The hospital first opened in 1910. On the left is the newer addition, built in 1948 at a cost of $800,000. Just to the right is the section built in 1925, and on its right, the section constructed in 1953. The hospital closed in 1972, and the facility became St. Catherine's Continuing Care Center.

The main track lines and depot (upper left) of the Chicago, Burlington and Quincy Railroad. The depot was located at 925 South 10th Street and first opened in 1898. An extensive remodeling was undertaken in 1929-30, and additional work was done on the exterior in 1954. All train service ended there on February 1, 1974, and the building was vacant for many years. Now, as "The Burlington," it is being restored and redeveloped for commercial and residential space. This photo was taken in August 1968.

In February 1966, the old Omaha City Hall building at the corner of 18th and Farnam streets was demolished. It had been built in 1890 and was one of the most elegant structures in Omaha. The original cost was $550,000. The southwest corner of the building held a 200-foot tower. This was partly taken down in 1919 when construction flaws appeared. The Public Safety Director officially classified the building as dangerous in 1962, and plans were made to replace it. The Woodmen Tower was built on the site.

Designed by Omaha architect Leo A. Daly, the new Woodmen Tower at 1700 Farnam Street stands tall in September 1968. The headquarters of the Woodmen of the World fraternal insurance company, founded in Omaha in 1890, was dedicated in 1969. The new structure became the "premier symbol" of the city, rising to a height of 30 stories (498 feet). It continues to serve the Woodmen of the World today and also provides office space for other tenants.

Notes on the Photographs

These notes, listed by page number, attempt to include all aspects known of the photographs. Each of the photographs is identified by the page number, a title or description, photographer and collection, archive, and call or box number when applicable. Although every attempt was made to collect all data, in some cases complete data may have been unavailable due to the age and condition of some of the photographs and records.

ii **Birds-eye View of Omaha High School**
Omaha Public Library
alb002_005

vi **The Exposition Building and Grand Opera House**
Omaha Public Library
pho_487

x **Union Station at 10th and Mason**
From the Bostwick-Frohardt Collection, owned by KM3TV and on permanent loan to Durham Western Heritage Museum, Omaha, Nebraska
31-782

2 **Missouri River Transfer Company**
Omaha Public Library
alb002_005

3 **Caldwell Block**
Omaha Public Library
pho_050

4 **Douglas Street**
From the Bostwick-Frohardt Collection, owned by KM3TV and on permanent loan to Durham Western Heritage Museum, Omaha, Nebraska
14-67

5 **Territorial Capitol**
Omaha Public Library
alb001_049e

6 **Missouri River Bridge**
Omaha Public Library
alb002_013

7 **The Tremont House**
Omaha Public Library
pho_153b

8 **City Hotel**
Omaha Public Library
pho_150

9 **Julius A. Roeder Drugstore**
Omaha Public Library
pho_151

10 **Metz Brothers Beer Hall**
Omaha Public Library
pho_152

11 **Omaha to the Northwest, 1879**
Omaha Public Library
alb001_044

12 **Paxton Hotel**
Omaha Public Library
ster_001

13 **Creighton College**
Omaha Public Library
pho_025

14 **The Sheely Block**
Omaha Public Library
pho_030

16 **Omaha High School**
Omaha Public Library
pho_024

17 **Douglas County Court House**
Omaha Public Library
pho_458

18 **President Benjamin Harrison in Omaha**
Omaha Public Library
pho_402

19 **Bridge Across the Missouri**
Omaha Public Library
pho_072

20 **Post Office**
Omaha Public Library
pho_477

21 **Millard Hotel**
Omaha Public Library
pho_027

22 **Executive Officers of the Trans-Mississippi Exposition**
Omaha Public Library
pho_183

23 **Residences in the "Gold Coast"**
Omaha Public Library
1s_00049

24 **United States Post Office**
Omaha Public Library
pho_103

25 **Larson's Store**
Omaha Public Library
pho_200

26 **Woodman and Ritchie Company**
Omaha Public Library
pho_037

27 **Portable Bandstand**
Omaha Public Library
pho_418

28 **Klopp, Bartlett and Company**
Omaha Public Library
pho_065

29 **Concert Pavilion**
Omaha Public Library
pho_415

30 **Farnam Street**
Omaha Public Library
1s_00008

31 **St. John's Collegiate Church**
Omaha Public Library
1s_00033

32 **Neighborhood Grocery Store**
Omaha Public Library
pho_404

33 **Lowering the Falconer Residence**
Omaha Public Library
1s_00125

34 **Street-Lowering Project**
Omaha Public Library
1s_00130

35 **Street Regrading**
Omaha Public Library
1s_00138

36 **Cavalry Maneuvers**
Omaha Public Library
1s_00147

37 **Horses at Fort Omaha**
Omaha Public Library
1s_00144

38 **Government Building**
Omaha Public Library
TMI00041

39 **Mini Roller Coaster**
Omaha Public Library
TMI00355

40 **Agricultural Building, Entrance**
Omaha Public Library
TMI00001

41 **General Electric Exhibition**
Omaha Public Library
TMI00183

42 **North Midway**
Omaha Public Library
TMI00228

43 **Great Naval Fight Cyclorama**
Omaha Public Library
TMI00373

44 **Blatz Beer Display**
Omaha Public Library
TMI00070

45 **Decorated Carriage**
Omaha Public Library
TMI00326

46 **Giant See-Saw**
Omaha Public Library
TMI00048

47 **American Wringer Company Exhibit**
Omaha Public Library
TMI00204

48 **Streets of Cairo Cafe**
Omaha Public Library
TMI00095

49 **Streets of All Nations**
Omaha Public Library
TMI00290

50 **Chief of Guards and Staff**
Omaha Public Library
TMI00337

51 **Indian Congress Parade**
Omaha Public Library
TMI00313

52 **Lake Nakoma**
Omaha Public Library
pho_410

54 **South from 15th and Dodge Streets**
Omaha Public Library
1s_00016

55 **O Street Viaduct**
From the Bostwick-Frohardt Collection, owned by KM3TV and on permanent loan to Durham Western Heritage Museum, Omaha, Nebraska
25-A1

56 **Omaha National Bank**
Omaha Public Library
1s_00024

57 **The Pavilion at Elmwood Park**
Omaha Public Library
pho_432

58 **Paxton Block**
Omaha Public Library
pho_249

59 **Pavilion at Riverside Park**
Omaha Public Library
pho_451

60 **Pavilion at Riverside Park no. 2**
Omaha Public Library
pho_452

61 **Crowd at Riverside Park Around 1905**
Omaha Public Library
pho_476

62 **Looking East Down Farnam Street**
Omaha Public Library
1s_00012

63 **Paving South 24th Street**
From the Bostwick-Frohardt Collection, owned by KM3TV and on permanent loan to Durham Western Heritage Museum, Omaha, Nebraska
6153-664

64 **Omaha National Bank**
Omaha Public Library
1s_00215

65 **Downtown Omaha**
Omaha Public Library
pho_144

66 **Fort Omaha Balloon School**
Omaha Public Library
1s_00152

67 **Elmwood Park, 1910**
Omaha Public Library
pho_420

68 **Lily Pond in Riverview Park**
Omaha Public Library
pho_444

69 **The Guarantee Laundry**
Omaha Public Library
pho_297

70 **New York Life Building**
Omaha Public Library
pho_056

71 **1913 Tornado**
From the Bostwick-Frohardt Collection, owned by KM3TV and on permanent loan to Durham Western Heritage Museum, Omaha, Nebraska
397-12

72 **Union Stockyards**
From the Bostwick-Frohardt Collection, owned by KM3TV and on permanent loan to Durham Western Heritage Museum, Omaha, Nebraska
25-11

73 **West on Farnam Street**
Omaha Public Library
1s_00015

74 **Miller Park**
Omaha Public Library
pho_467

75 **Elmwood Park Golf Course**
Omaha Public Library
pho_431a

76 **Blackstone Hotel**
Omaha Public Library
pho_049

77 **Old City Hall**
From the Bostwick-Frohardt Collection, owned by KM3TV and on permanent loan to Durham Western Heritage Museum, Omaha, Nebraska
61-73

78 **AK-SAR-BEN Parade**
From the Bostwick-Frohardt Collection, owned by KM3TV and on permanent loan to Durham Western Heritage Museum, Omaha, Nebraska
771-102

79 **AK-SAR-BEN Float**
From the Bostwick-Frohardt Collection, owned by KM3TV and on permanent loan to Durham Western Heritage Museum, Omaha, Nebraska
771-80

80 **North-northwest from the Top of the Woodmen of the World Building**
From the Bostwick-Frohardt Collection, owned by KM3TV and on permanent loan to Durham Western Heritage Museum, Omaha, Nebraska
15-213

82 **Excavation for the Medical Arts Building**
From the Bostwick-Frohardt Collection, owned by KM3TV and on permanent loan to Durham Western Heritage Museum, Omaha, Nebraska
1933-19

83 **AK-SAR-BEN**
From the Bostwick-Frohardt Collection, owned by KM3TV and on permanent loan to Durham Western Heritage Museum, Omaha, Nebraska
771-380

84 **Fontenelle Hotel**
From the Bostwick-Frohardt Collection, owned by KM3TV and on permanent loan to Durham Western Heritage Museum, Omaha, Nebraska
506-348

85 **Livestock Exchange Building**
From the Bostwick-Frohardt Collection, owned by KM3TV and on permanent loan to Durham Western Heritage Museum, Omaha, Nebraska
25-467

86 **Dundee Theatre**
From the Bostwick-Frohardt Collection, owned by KM3TV and on permanent loan to Durham Western Heritage Museum, Omaha, Nebraska
3325-1

87 **Lake George**
From the Bostwick-Frohardt Collection, owned by KM3TV and on permanent loan to Durham Western Heritage Museum, Omaha, Nebraska
15-320

88 **Dodge Street East from 14th Street**
From the Bostwick-Frohardt Collection, owned by KM3TV and on permanent loan to Durham Western Heritage Museum, Omaha, Nebraska
15-217

89 **16th and Dodge Streets, 1921**
From the Bostwick-Frohardt Collection, owned by KM3TV and on permanent loan to Durham Western Heritage Museum, Omaha, Nebraska
15-231

90 **Howard Street West from 8th Street**
From the Bostwick-Frohardt Collection, owned by KM3TV and on permanent loan to Durham Western Heritage Museum, Omaha, Nebraska
61-22

91 **East on Farnam Street from the Blackstone Hotel**
From the Bostwick-Frohardt Collection, owned by KM3TV and on permanent loan to Durham Western Heritage Museum, Omaha, Nebraska
61-142

92 **16th Street at Jackson**
From the Bostwick-Frohardt Collection, owned by KM3TV and on permanent loan to Durham Western Heritage Museum, Omaha, Nebraska
60-225

93 **Butter-Nut Coffee**
From the Bostwick-Frohardt Collection, owned by KM3TV and on permanent loan to Durham Western Heritage Museum, Omaha, Nebraska
426-135

94 **Racetrack**
From the Bostwick-Frohardt Collection, owned by KM3TV and on permanent loan to Durham Western Heritage Museum, Omaha, Nebraska
771-393

95 **North on 15th Street from Carlton Hotel**
From the Bostwick-Frohardt Collection, owned by KM3TV and on permanent loan to Durham Western Heritage Museum, Omaha, Nebraska
3496-20

96 **Bar and Café**
From the Bostwick-Frohardt Collection, owned by KM3TV and on permanent loan to Durham Western Heritage Museum, Omaha, Nebraska
5881-1

97 **Union Station**
From the Bostwick-Frohardt Collection, owned by KM3TV and on permanent loan to Durham Western Heritage Museum, Omaha, Nebraska
31-764

98 **Baum Drug Company Cars**
From the Wentworth Collection. Owned by Durham Western Heritage Museum, Omaha, Nebraska
WW335-1

99 **Walgreen's Drug Store**
From the Wentworth Collection. Owned by Durham Western Heritage Museum, Omaha, Nebraska
WW361-1.04

100 **Tire Store**
From the Wentworth Collection. Owned by Durham Western Heritage Museum, Omaha, Nebraska
WW328-1

101 **Orpheum Theatre**
From the Wentworth Collection. Owned by Durham Western Heritage Museum, Omaha, Nebraska
WW104-16.01

102 **Orpheum Theatre Posters**
From the Wentworth Collection. Owned by Durham Western Heritage Museum, Omaha, Nebraska
WW86-21.01

103 **Warehouse Building at 711 South 11th Street**
From the Wentworth Collection. Owned by Durham Western Heritage Museum, Omaha, Nebraska
WW85.1

104 **Harkert's**
From the Wentworth Collection. Owned by Durham Western Heritage Museum, Omaha, Nebraska
WW54-3.05

105 **McFayden Stewart**
From the Wentworth Collection. Owned by Durham Western Heritage Museum, Omaha, Nebraska
WW145-23

106 **Technical High School Band**
From the Wentworth Collection. Owned by Durham Western Heritage Museum, Omaha, Nebraska
WW5T-47

107 **Barnsdall Symphony Orchestra**
From the Bostwick-Frohardt Collection, owned by KM3TV and on permanent loan to Durham Western Heritage Museum, Omaha, Nebraska
3622-139

108 **Happy Hollow Club**
From the Bostwick-Frohardt Collection, owned by KM3TV and on permanent loan to Durham Western Heritage Museum, Omaha, Nebraska
47-104

110 **Glaser's Provisions**
From the Bostwick-Frohardt Collection, owned by KM3TV and on permanent loan to Durham Western Heritage Museum, Omaha, Nebraska
5600-30

111 **Petersen and Michelsen Hardware Store**
From the Bostwick-Frohardt Collection, owned by KM3TV and on permanent loan to Durham Western Heritage Museum, Omaha, Nebraska
3452-23

112 **Roseland Theater**
From the Bostwick-Frohardt Collection, owned by KM3TV and on permanent loan to Durham Western Heritage Museum, Omaha, Nebraska
6369-1

113 **Army Day at Fort Omaha**
From the Bostwick-Frohardt Collection, owned by KM3TV and on permanent loan to Durham Western Heritage Museum, Omaha, Nebraska
3622-247

114 **V-J Day**
From the Bostwick-Frohardt Collection, owned by KM3TV and on permanent loan to Durham Western Heritage Museum, Omaha, Nebraska
4820-40

115 **Candidate Thomas Dewey Interview on KOIL**
From the Bostwick-Frohardt Collection, owned by KM3TV and on permanent loan to Durham Western Heritage Museum, Omaha, Nebraska
3622-252

116 **Nat Towles Great Orchestra**
From the Bostwick-Frohardt Collection, owned by KM3TV and on permanent loan to Durham Western Heritage Museum, Omaha, Nebraska
5645-7

117 **President Harry S. Truman at Boys Town**
From the Bostwick-Frohardt Collection, owned by KM3TV and on permanent loan to Durham Western Heritage Museum, Omaha, Nebraska
4820-53.02

118 **Harney Street**
From the Bostwick-Frohardt Collection, owned by KM3TV and on permanent loan to Durham Western Heritage Museum, Omaha, Nebraska
6387-5

119 **Engineering Project**
From the Bostwick-Frohardt Collection, owned by KM3TV and on permanent loan to Durham Western Heritage Museum, Omaha, Nebraska
6340-29

120 **North from 16th and Harney**
From the Bostwick-Frohardt Collection, owned by KM3TV and on permanent loan to Durham Western Heritage Museum, Omaha, Nebraska
358-261

121 **S. S. Kresge Company Store**
From the Bostwick-Frohardt Collection, owned by KM3TV and on permanent loan to Durham Western Heritage Museum, Omaha, Nebraska
358-263

122 **Hanscom Park Methodist Church Building**
From the Bostwick-Frohardt Collection, owned by KM3TV and on permanent loan to Durham Western Heritage Museum, Omaha, Nebraska
5333-7

123 **Craddock's Bicycle Shop**
From the Bostwick-Frohardt Collection, owned by KM3TV and on permanent loan to Durham Western Heritage Museum, Omaha, Nebraska
61-264

124 **South 24th and N Streets**
From the Bostwick-Frohardt Collection, owned by KM3TV and on permanent loan to Durham Western Heritage Museum, Omaha, Nebraska
6153-799

125 **Missouri River Flood**
From the Bostwick-Frohardt Collection, owned by KM3TV and on permanent loan to Durham Western Heritage Museum, Omaha, Nebraska
4820-52

126 **Aerial Shot of Downtown, 1955**
From the Bostwick-Frohardt Collection, owned by KM3TV and on permanent loan to Durham Western Heritage Museum, Omaha, Nebraska
4937-2

127 **St. Catherine's Hospital**
Durham Western Heritage Museum
7004-5

128 **Chicago, Burlington and Quincy Railroad**
Durham Western Heritage Museum
7011-47

129 **Razing of Old City Hall**
Durham Western Heritage Museum
7008-4.01

130 **New Woodmen Tower**
Durham Western Heritage Museum
7003-29